A Scare in the City

by Sherilin Chanek

Illustrated by Rudy Gutierrez

HAMPTON-BROWN

It's Monday morning in the big city. Some people are already working. Many more people are on their way to work.

At 211 Delaware Street, two window cleaners stand on a platform outside the tenth floor. The radio plays as they do their chores.

Inside, a doctor shares an elevator with a painter. They are each going to work.

In the store at 200 Delaware Street, a store clerk uses a cash register to add up what the shoppers owe.

In an apartment above the store, a police officer snores in bed. He sleeps late because he works at night.

On the street in front of the store, many cars wait for the red traffic light to turn green.

Many more people are traveling to work on a train. The train goes into a tunnel.

It's a normal Monday morning.

All of a sudden the traffic lights go dark. The elevator stops. The train slows to a stop in the tunnel.

"What's happening?" someone gasps.

A news reporter on the radio explains.

"There is some trouble in the city today. At exactly 8:28 this morning, the city lost all electric power. Electric workers are working to fix the wires and restore the power. As soon as we know more, we will tell you."

A man on the train with a radio shares this news with his neighbors.

The mayor and the fire chief meet at City Hall. In the street, a siren blares. It is the police chief on his way. These leaders will help to keep their neighbors safe until power is restored. They will call extra workers to help them with their plan.

Snore, snore. The police officer is still sleeping. His alarm clock did not go off because it is electric. Ring, ring! It is not the clock. It is a phone call from his supervisor.

"Can you come into work right now? The power is out. The police chief needs extra people to direct traffic."

The police officer agrees because he cares about his neighbors.

A 9-1-1 operator is at work. She takes calls from people who are in trouble. A call comes in.

"Hello. We're stuck in an elevator at 211 Delaware Street!"

"I will connect your call to the fire department. Firefighters will help you. It may be a while before they arrive because the power is out in the whole city."

"It's lucky I had my phone," the doctor says. "I keep it with me in case someone is in trouble and needs to find me. I didn't know I would be the one in trouble today."

The painter just grins. It does not look as if he's going to finish his work today.

A teacher reads to his class by light from the classroom window. As they hear the story, the children don't feel scared.

The window cleaners can't wash any more windows because they are stuck. Their platform cannot move up or down until the power is restored. People on the street stare up at them. The window cleaners wave.

Still stuck inside the elevator, the doctor and painter tell stories about their jobs. They make jokes. That way they don't get bored.

The store clerk uses a paper and pen to add up what the shoppers owe. She is good at math. She shows the shoppers the numbers with a flashlight.

The train is still stuck in the tunnel. Some riders sit on the floor. One rider turns to her neighbors. "Would you like to share these muffins?" she asks.

One person says, "Yes. Thank you. I'm ready for a morning snack."

The police officer is out directing traffic. He stops cars to let a fire truck go by.

At 211 Delaware Street a banker opens a window on the tenth floor. The window cleaners climb inside. They thank the banker.

"I wouldn't dare work on a platform up so high," the banker says. "I would be scared."

"We're used to it. It's our job," the window cleaners say.

Police help the people in the train form a line and walk out of the tunnel. The people are late for work, but they are all safe. They have a good story to tell.

Firefighters help the doctor and painter get out of the elevator. The doctor and painter trade phone numbers. They are friends now and make plans to call each other soon.

School is over for the day. The children get on the school bus. The bus driver will be careful. Neighbors come out to direct traffic so there will be no trouble.

The electric workers find out what's wrong with the wires. The power will be restored before long.

3:16 P.M.

The power comes back on. Hooray! The scare is over.

Many workers are tired because they worked so hard to help their neighbors, but they are happy. If there is trouble again, they will know what to do.